Ian Wilkinson was born and raised in Sunderland in the north-east of England. Following many adventures after studying at the University of Sussex, he eventually became a further education lecturer working and residing in London. Having travelled extensively in his youth, he now explores the world of his imagination while living in South London.

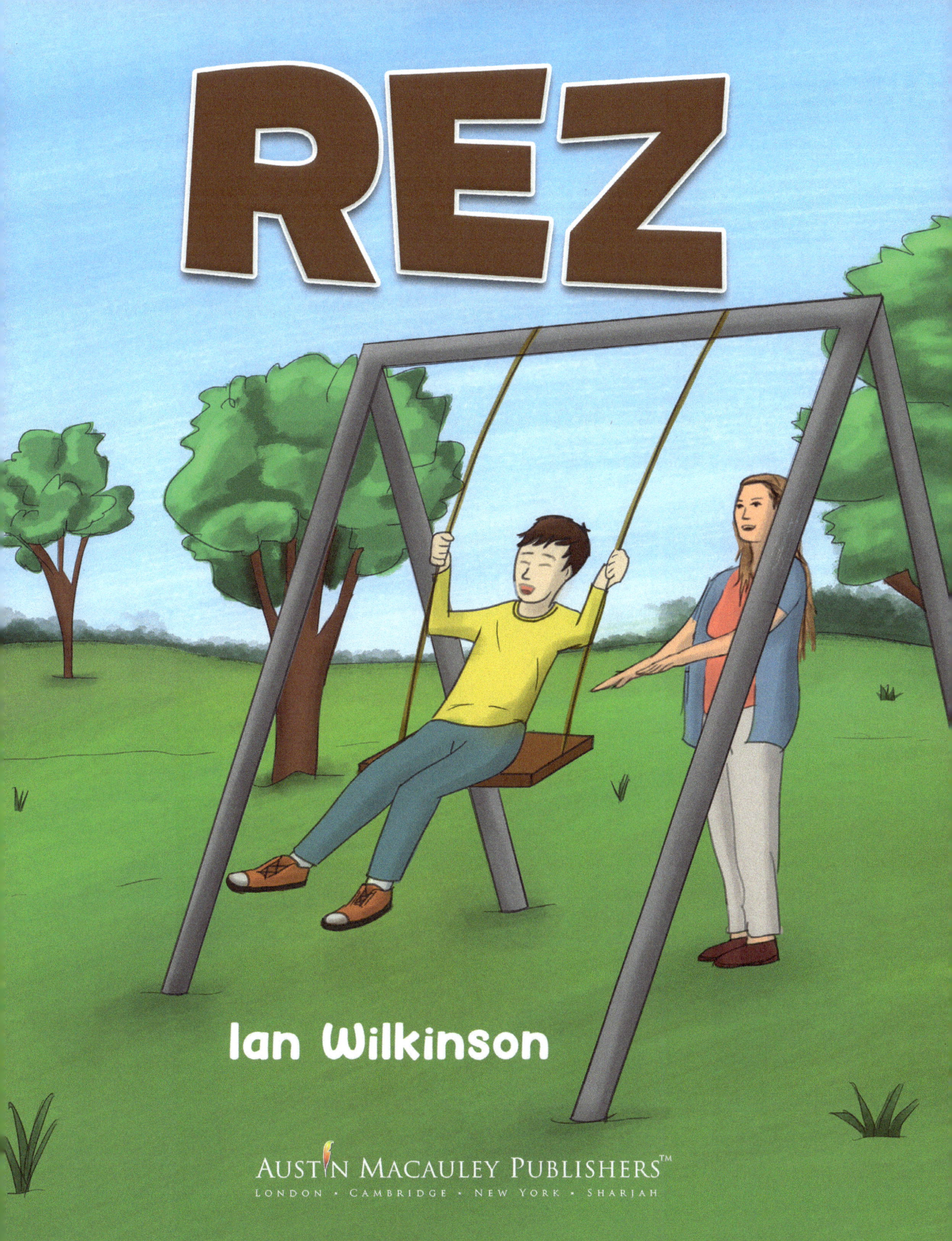

Copyright © Ian Wilkinson 2024

The right of **Ian Wilkinson** to be identified as author of this work has been asserted by the author in accordance with sections 77 and 78 of the Copyright, Designs and Patents Act 1988.

All rights reserved. No part of this publication may be reproduced, stored in a retrieval system, or transmitted in any form or by any means, electronic, mechanical, photocopying, recording, or otherwise, without the prior permission of the publishers.

Any person who commits any unauthorised act in relation to this publication may be liable to criminal prosecution and civil claims for damages.

A CIP catalogue record for this title is available from the British Library.

ISBN 9781035807796 (Paperback)

ISBN 9781035807802 (ePub e-book)

www.austinmacauley.co.uk

First Published 2024

Austin Macauley Publishers Ltd®

1 Canada Square

Canary Wharf

London

E14 5AA

This book is dedicated to all who have experienced loss.

I would like to thank the staff at the production, editing and marketing departments at Austin Macauley Publishers for all their advice and guidance during the publishing process.

A special thank you also to the illustrator for providing drawings that helped to bring the story to life.

Particular gratitude goes to my children, Tom and Ellen, for allowing me to have the privilege of being their parent. Finally, my thanks go to Catherine for all her love, support and encouragement over the years.

Rez had finally stopped crying. They felt scared because they had never experienced crying like that before. Their whole body had been shaking and it felt as if they had lost control of themself. There was now a wet patch on the pillow and the sheets had become messy and crumpled.

Rez had been living with their Mum, who had given birth to Rez, and Mum's partner whom Rez called Mam. Mum had recently died, and the funeral had been held that day. Rez had gone to bed but had become very upset when trying to go to sleep,

thinking of Mum and that they would never be with her ever again. Rez was 11 years old and was about to begin studying at a new school.

Mam came into the room and sat on a chair next to Rez's bed.

"How are you feeling?" Mam asked.
"I wish Mum was still here." Rez replied.
"I know, I wish she was too."
"I'm worried that I'm always going to feel as sad as I do now."
"You won't always feel as bad as you are feeling now, but you will always feel a bit sad when you think of Mum. It is just a part of being human; to miss the people you love
when they are no longer here. But there will also be times when you feel happy remembering the lovely times you shared together."
"I'm also worried that I'm going to die, just like Mum."
"It's only natural to feel like that but remember that you are not the same person as Mum. You are a unique combination of genes that have been passed down by people over thousands of years. There only ever has been and there only ever will be one you."

"But I'm never going to see Mum again?"

"No, I can't tell you that you are going to see her again but in some ways she lives on inside you and in your memories of her. One day you might decide and may be able to pass your genes on to another human being and Mum will also live on in that way too. That might be with someone you love who has a different type of body to yours, or else it might be someone with the same kind of body as yours. Or you may decide to have a child and raise it by yourself or perhaps adopt a child that needs to be looked after. You might also decide that you don't want to have or adopt any children at all. It doesn't really matter, what matters is that you do what feels right for you inside."

"Remember that your body has a certain shape but that shouldn't define who you are as a person. You don't have to be or feel or do something just because that is what is expected of people with bodies like yours. Always ask yourself why you think this is expected of you and is it something that you feel is right for you. Be true to yourself. Be yourself. Be you."

"The important thing is that you are a person, a human being, not a particular kind of human being just because your body happens to have certain characteristics."

"All that you can know is that you are a human being who is alive on this planet alongside billions of other human beings, animals and plants, and that you have a right to experience that life just as much as they do. Whenever you are feeling anxious or worried just try to remember that, and that you should live your life to the full until it comes to a natural end."

"I know you like to be called Rez but what is your full first name?" asked Mam.
"Resilience," replied Rez.
"And what does resilience mean?"
"It means being able to withstand the difficulties that you experience during your life, and to keep on going in spite of them."
"And why did Mum and I decide to name you that?"
"Because you both thought that it is the most important quality a human being can have throughout their lives."
"Exactly. We just didn't think that you would need it so soon…"
At this point, Mam began crying in the way that Rez had been crying earlier before she came into the room. Rez stroked her head as she sobbed uncontrollably. In a strange way, it was comforting for Rez to see someone else crying in this way as it made them realise that this was just a natural human response to losing someone you love.

Eventually Mam stopped crying. Both she and Rez managed to laugh at the fact that crying also means having a very runny nose as Mam took a tissue to blow hers.

At this point, Mam gave Rez a kiss and a hug and said goodnight before leaving the room.

Rez turned off the bedside light and laid in bed thinking of Mum and about what Mam had said. Even though they still felt very sad and knew that this was a sadness that would be within them forever, they also knew that it was important to keep on living and to try and take the best out of each day for the rest of their life.

The End

Milton Keynes UK
Ingram Content Group UK Ltd.
UKHW052205271123
433355UK00009B/312